Country File
Japan

Michael March

W
FRANKLIN WATTS
LONDON•SYDNEY

First published in 2003 by
Franklin Watts
96 Leonard Street, London
EC2A 4XD

Franklin Watts Australia
45–51 Huntley Street,
Alexandria, NSW 2015

COUNTRY FILE: JAPAN produced for Franklin Watts by
Bender Richardson White, PO Box 266, Uxbridge, UK.
Editor: Lionel Bender
Designer and Page Make-up: Ben White
Picture Researcher: Cathy Stastny
Cover Make-up: Mike Pilley, Radius
Production: Kim Richardson

Graphics and Maps: Stefan Chabluk

Consultant: Dr Terry Jennings, a former geography teacher
and university lecturer. He is now a full-time writer of
children's geography and science books.

A CIP catalogue record for this book is available
from the British Library.

ISBN 0-7496-4814-7

Manufactured in China

Picture Credits
Pages 1: Japanese Information and Cultural Centre.
3: PhotoDisc Inc/Jeremy Hoare. 4: Eye Ubiquitous/David
Forman. 7: Corbis Images/Michael S. Yamashita.
9: Japanese Information and Cultural Centre.
10: PhotoDisc Inc/Jeremy Hoare. 11. Eye
Ubiquitous/David Forman. 12: James Davis Travel
Photography. 13: Eye Ubiquitous/Frank Leather. 15: Eye
Ubiquitous/Frank Leather. 16: Japanese Information and
Cultural Centre. 17: Eye Ubiquitous/R.Haynes.
18: Japanese Information and Cultural Centre.
19: Japanese Information and Cultural Centre. 20: Eye
Ubiquitous/Frank Leather. 21: Eye Ubiquitous/John
Dakers. 22 top: Eye Ubiquitous/Frank Leather.
22 bottom: Eye Ubiquitous/Paul Seheult. 24: Japanese
Information and Cultural Centre. 25: Eye
Ubiquitous/Trisha Rafferty. 26: James Davis Travel
Photography. 27: Japanese Information and Cultural
Centre. 28: Eye Ubiquitous/Adina Tovy-Amsel. 29: Eye
Ubiquitous/Paul Seheult. 30: Japanese Information and
Cultural Centre. 31: PhotoDisc Inc/Geostock.

Cover Photo: James Davis Travel Photography.

The Author
Michael March is a full-time writer and
editor of non-fiction books. He has
written more than 15 books for children
about different countries of the world.

Contents

Welcome to Japan

Japan lies off the east coast of mainland Asia. It is made up of a chain of rugged islands some 2,400 kilometres long that curves north-eastward across the Pacific Ocean. According to legend, it was put there as a gift from the gods. Japanese people call their country Nippon, meaning 'land of the rising sun'.

The Sea of Japan separates the island nation of Japan from the Korean peninsula to the west. To the south-west, across the East China Sea, is the long coastline of China. Russia, another huge neighbour, lies to the north.

Four main islands

Many of Japan's 4,000 or so islands are tiny. The four main islands – Honshu, Hokkaido, Kyushu and Shikoku – occupy more than 99 per cent of the 378,000 square kilometres that make up the land mass. Most Japanese people live on Honshu, the biggest of the islands.

View over the city and bay of Tokyo. In the background is the Rainbow Bridge, leading to Odeiba island. ▼

The Land

Plants and Animals

Chrysanthemum (the national flower), azalea, lotus, lily and cherry blossom are a few of Japan's many flowering plants. Bamboo and mangrove forests grow in the south, spruce and larch in the north, and beech and willow in central Japan.

Animals include the red-faced macaque, badgers, foxes, bears, bats, deer, mink, seals, giant salamanders and sea snakes.

Japan is a land of mostly high mountains and narrow valleys with rivers. Much of the soil is volcanic, producing hot springs. Only a little over one-eighth of the terrain is suitable for growing crops. Most Japanese people live on the coastal plains or lower slopes, where transport and farming are easier.

At 3,776 metres, snow-capped Mount Fuji, on Honshu, is Japan's highest peak. The mountain, which is a dormant volcano, is sacred to the Japanese. Its beauty has inspired artists and poets down the ages. Fuji (shown on the book cover) has not erupted for nearly 300 years, but more than forty of Japan's many volcanoes are still active.

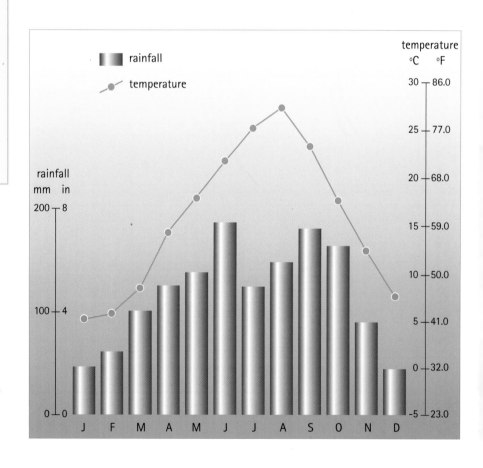

Rainfall and temperature graph for Tokyo, on Honshu, where summers are warm and winters mild. Islands to the south have a sub-tropical climate: it is warmer all year round. Hokkaido has a sub-arctic climate, with mild summers and cold, snowy winters. ▶▶

Earthquakes and tidal waves

Earthquakes are frequent in Japan and, if severe, do great harm. In 1995, a mighty earthquake struck the town of Kobe, on Honshu, killing over 6,000 people. Tsunamis – tidal waves that build up from the ocean floor – sometimes accompany the earthquakes to threaten coastal areas.

Climate

In summer and autumn, the coast is often battered by violent storms called typhoons. These can cause flooding and mudslides. Summers are hot and humid with plenty of rain, except on the northern island of Hokkaido, where it is cooler and drier. There, winters can be so cold that the sea freezes over. Across the country, spring brings with it warmer weather, and in April people look forward to the cherry trees coming into flower, when they hold cherry blossom parties to mark the occasion.

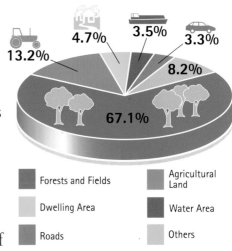

13.2% 4.7% 3.5% 3.3%
8.2%
67.1%

■ Forests and Fields	■ Agricultural Land
■ Dwelling Area	■ Water Area
■ Roads	■ Others

▲ So much land is mountainous or covered in forest that less than one-fifth of the country can be used as farmland or land for housing the population.

◀◀ Flat land suitable for agriculture is intensively used, such as this field of tea plants, in Kagoshima on Kyushu. The tea is being picked and put into baskets. It is a highly valued crop.

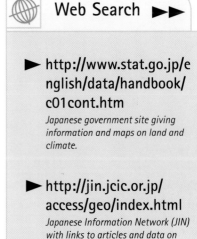

Web Search ▶▶

▶ http://www.stat.go.jp/english/data/handbook/c01cont.htm
Japanese government site giving information and maps on land and climate.

▶ http://jin.jcic.or.jp/access/geo/index.html
Japanese Information Network (JIN) with links to articles and data on land and climate.

The People

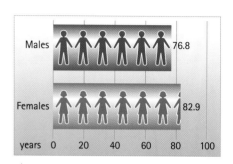

Japanese women can look forward to surviving into their 80s while men, on average, will live only till their late 70s.

With some 127 million people, Japan has the eighth-largest population in the world. The Japanese are partly descended from people who long ago crossed over from the Asian mainland to settle the islands, where they mixed with the local people.

Other early ancestors of the Japanese were Pacific islanders who came from the south. Later, Koreans and Chinese arrived. By the end of the 1st century CE, the people on the islands now known as Japan resembled the present-day inhabitants and spoke a language not unlike the Japanese that is spoken there now. In Japan today, Koreans are the biggest national minority group, although they make up only 0.6 per cent of the population. The Chinese are the next biggest.

DATABASE

The Japanese language

Japanese was first written down in the 5th century CE, using Chinese characters, or symbols. Traditionally, Japanese is written downwards, in columns, starting from the right-hand side. Nowadays, it is also written across the page, from left to right. Modern Japanese uses about 2,000 Chinese characters, which represent meanings rather than sounds. It also uses other characters, which, like letters of the English alphabet, stand for sounds.

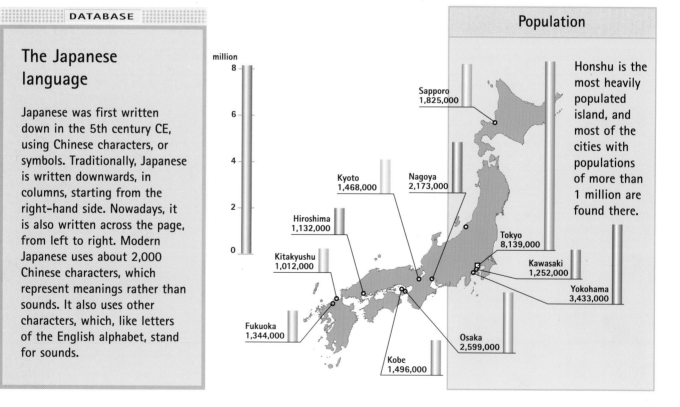

Population

Honshu is the most heavily populated island, and most of the cities with populations of more than 1 million are found there.

Sapporo 1,825,000

Kyoto 1,468,000

Nagoya 2,173,000

Hiroshima 1,132,000

Tokyo 8,139,000

Kawasaki 1,252,000

Kitakyushu 1,012,000

Yokohama 3,433,000

Fukuoka 1,344,000

Osaka 2,599,000

Kobe 1,496,000

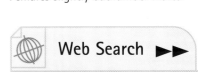
Breakfast time in the home of a modern Japanese family.

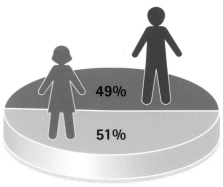

49%

51%

Female Population 64,707,500	Male Population 62,064,150

Japan has more boys than girls, and more men than women, in all the age groups up to the late 40s. From age 50 and over, women outnumber men. Females slightly outnumber males.

A changing population

The Ainu, a people who were among the earliest settlers, are far fewer in number now and live mainly on Hokkaido. They are ethnically distinct from other Japanese people and have their own culture. However, over the centuries, many Ainu have intermarried with the Japanese and adopted their way of life and their traditions.

Most of Japan's population is between 20 and 60, with people in their fifties making up the biggest age group. The second-biggest group are the twenty-somethings. In recent times, the over-70s group has increased greatly.

Language

Japanese is the one and only official language. The written language is the same all over Japan, but pronunciation differs across the country and each region has its own dialect words. The standard form of spoken Japanese is as it is spoken in Tokyo, the nation's capital.

Web Search ▶▶

▶ http://education.yahoo.com/reference/factbook/ja/popula.html
Information on Japan's population.

▶ www.stat.go.jp/english/data/handbook/c02cont.htm#cha2_6jin.jcic.or.jp/general.html
Population guide from Japan Statistics Bureau site .

Urban and Rural Life

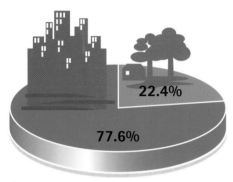

22.4%

77.6%

■ Percentage of Population
Living in Urban Areas

■ Percentage of Population
Living in Rural Areas

▲▲ Less than a quarter of Japanese people live in the countryside. Most of these are farmers.

Modern city centres are filled with high-rise offices, apartment buildings, shops and hotels. This is the centre of Tokyo. ▼▼

Japan is one of the most densely populated countries in the world. It has an average of more than 300 people living on every square kilometre of land. Nearly eight out of ten Japanese inhabit the big towns and cities or their suburbs. Fewer and fewer people are living in rural areas.

Although Japan's population continues to grow, the growth rate is slowing down and is expected to fall well below one-tenth of 1 per cent by 2010. About a quarter of the present population lives in or around Tokyo, the country's bustling capital and its biggest city by far. Tokyo, Yokohama, its neighbour and the second-biggest city, and Osaka, the third-biggest, all lie on the crowded coastal plains of Honshu.

Small houses, high-rise flats

Especially in urban areas, land is in short supply and is very expensive. Most town-dwellers live in small houses or in high-rise blocks of flats. Modern houses are made of steel and concrete as well as wood.

A traditional Japanese house and outbuildings. Such wooden buildings were once put together without using nails or screws.

Traditional houses, hot baths

In rural areas, the houses are often bigger and built in the traditional style. On entering, Japanese people remove their shoes and put on slippers. The floors are covered with rush matting called *tatami*. People sit on cushions on the floor and sleep on a padded mattress called a *futon*.

Sliding paper screens serve as doors separating the rooms. The screens can be removed in hot weather to create a through draught. In the bathroom, a square bathtub is used for bathing, not washing. Japanese people wash themselves with soap and water before getting into the tub, so that the clean bathwater can be used by other family members.

Web Search ▶▶

▶ http://www.jinjapan.org/kidsweb/japan/a.html
Kidsweb Japan site with information for children on daily life in Japan.

▶ http://www.jinjapan.org/atlas/communities/commun_fr.html
Site giving information on different communities in Japan.

▶ http://jin.jcic.or.jp/leisure.html
Japanese Information Network (JIN) with links to articles on daily life.

Farming and Fishing

Japanese farms are quite small (usually under two hectares), but highly efficient. Some farmers harvest more than one rice crop a year. Fish, along with rice, is an essential part of the Japanese diet, so fishing, like farming, is an important industry.

Farmland was always scarce in Japan, and with the growth of the industrial cities the number of farms has steadily decreased. Today, only about 1 working person in 20 works on the land, and some farmers are only part-time. However, for their size Japanese farms are some of the most productive in the world. Their success is due to intensive farming techniques, improved seed varieties and machines such as rice planters and power cultivators.

A catch of tuna fish is being unloaded from a fishing vessel.

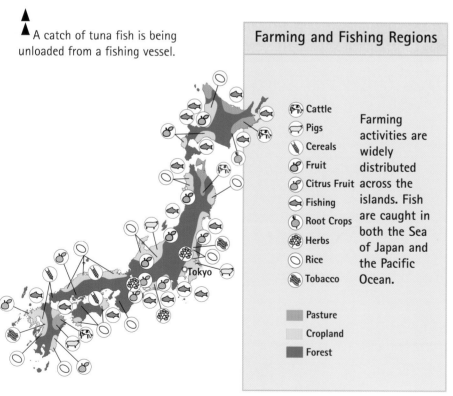

Farming and Fishing Regions

Cattle
Pigs
Cereals
Fruit
Citrus Fruit
Fishing
Root Crops
Herbs
Rice
Tobacco

Pasture
Cropland
Forest

Farming activities are widely distributed across the islands. Fish are caught in both the Sea of Japan and the Pacific Ocean.

Tokyo

Rice, fruit and beef

Although rice is still the main crop, Japanese farmers also grow other cereals, cabbages, potatoes, onions and other vegetables, a wide variety of fruit – including mandarin oranges, apples and melons – as well as soya beans, sugar cane, tea and tobacco. Some farms raise cattle, pigs and poultry for meat and dairy products. Beef from Kobe is famous throughout Japan. Extra meat, fruit and sugar cane are also imported.

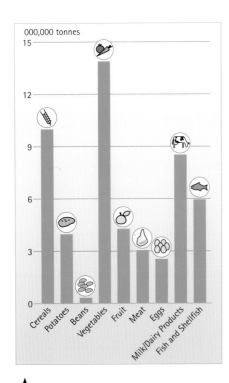

000,000 tonnes

Annual production by weight of crops, dairy produce, fish and shellfish.

Timber

Outside the farming areas, much of Japan is covered in forest. Wood is used for building, for papermaking and in many other products. However, the quantities of timber produced are insufficient for all Japan's needs and most of the wood that is used comes from abroad.

Fish and shellfish

Japan also imports about 40 per cent of the fish that its people eat. So great is the Japanese appetite for fish that even the Japanese fishing fleet, which lands about 15 per cent of the world's catch, cannot, by itself, meet that need. The catch includes bonito, squid, pollock, tuna, mackerel and other varieties. Many kinds of fish and shellfish, including oysters, along with edible seaweed are produced on fish farms in coastal bays.

Harvesting rice by machine near Kyoto. The grains of rice are loaded directly into sacks. ▼

Web Search ▶▶

▶ http://www.stat.go.jp/ english/data/handbook/ c05cont.htm

Japanese Statistics Bureau Statistical Handbook of Japan. Chapter on agriculture, forestry and fisheries.

▶ http://jin.jcic.or.jp/ business.html

Japanese Information Network (JIN) with links to articles and data on farming, forestry and fisheries.

Resources and Industry

DATABASE

Employment

Taken together, commerce and services, finance, insurance and real estate (buying and selling of land and buildings) account for more than half of Japan's workforce. Fewer people are employed in manufacturing, but some Japanese firms, such as Nissan and Sony, now also have factories abroad. The numbers working in farming, forestry and fishing have steadily declined and are relatively few.

F or a long time, Japan's prosperity has depended on the success of its manufacturing industries. However, in recent years, commerce and the service industries have overtaken manufacturing as the country's main employer and wealth creator.

To meet its manufacturing and energy needs, Japan has to import most of its fuel and raw materials. Some coal is mined on Hokkaido and Honshu, but the main fuel used is oil from the Middle East. The oil is shipped to Japan in giant tankers, many of which are Japanese-built. The steel used in the ship-construction yards is also made in Japan, but from imported ores. Japan is one of the top two shipbuilding and steelmaking nations.

Resources and Industry

Much of Japanese industry is concentrated in the big cities on the coastal plains.

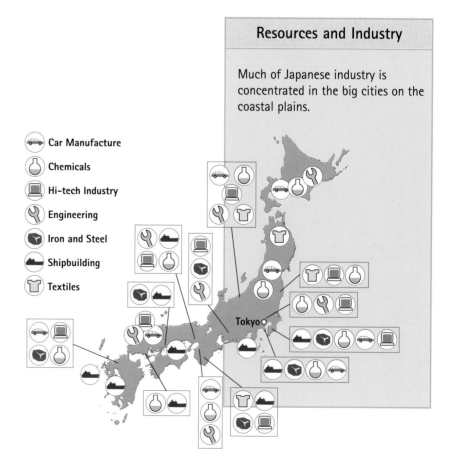

- Car Manufacture
- Chemicals
- Hi-tech Industry
- Engineering
- Iron and Steel
- Shipbuilding
- Textiles

▲ Warehouses, cranes and stacks of huge metal containers line the quayside at the port of Osaka.

Manufacturing

Japan is also one of the world's biggest producers of cars, motorcycles and other motor vehicles. The cars are built using robots and the latest assembly-line techniques. About half of all the vehicles produced are sold abroad, and some of the car firms also have overseas factories.

The electrical and electronics industries have been equally successful. Many of the televisions, cameras, camcorders, computers, mobile telephones and hi-fi components on sale on high streets across the world are Japanese. Other valuable exports include machine tools, chemicals, paints and textiles.

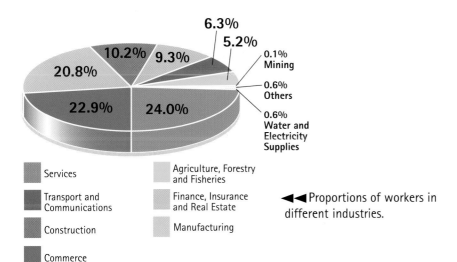

◄◄ Proportions of workers in different industries.

- Services
- Transport and Communications
- Construction
- Commerce
- Agriculture, Forestry and Fisheries
- Finance, Insurance and Real Estate
- Manufacturing

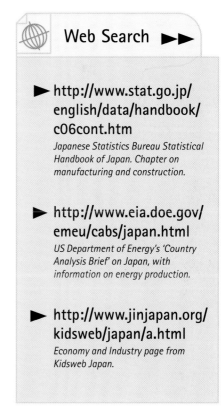

Web Search ►►

► http://www.stat.go.jp/english/data/handbook/c06cont.htm
Japanese Statistics Bureau Statistical Handbook of Japan. Chapter on manufacturing and construction.

► http://www.eia.doe.gov/emeu/cabs/japan.html
US Department of Energy's 'Country Analysis Brief' on Japan, with information on energy production.

► http://www.jinjapan.org/kidsweb/japan/a.html
Economy and Industry page from Kidsweb Japan.

Transport

A network of roads and railways crosses Japan, linked by bridges and tunnels. Ferries ply the waters between the islands while Japan's 173 airports handle a huge volume of internal and international flights. A large fleet of merchant ships operates out of Japan's seaports.

Japan has the best and fastest railway system in the world. On some routes the high-speed *shinkansen* (Bullet Train) averages more than 260 km/h. Six shinkansen lines, starting from Tokyo, serve towns as far away as Fukuoka, on Kyushu, in the south, and Morioka and Akita on northern Honshu. The high-speed trains always run on time and little but an earthquake can disrupt their schedules. Other train services connect with destinations that are not on the shinkansen routes.

Road traffic in Japan drives on the left, as in the United Kingdom and Australia. Drivers must pay a toll to use the fastest roads – the modern expressways. All other roads are free of charge, but some are closed in winter because of bad weather. Long-distance buses, operated by a variety of companies, run between the towns. Travel by bus is much cheaper than by train, but much slower.

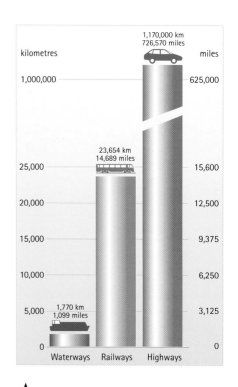

▲ Total length of main transport systems in Japan.

Multi-lane expressways link the major cities. ►►

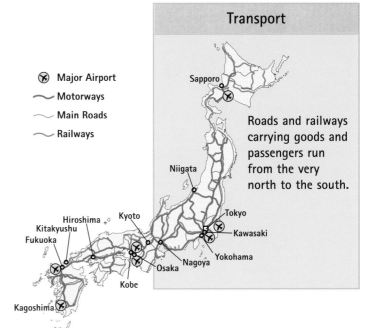

⊗ Major Airport
⌢ Motorways
⌢ Main Roads
⌢ Railways

Roads and railways carrying goods and passengers run from the very north to the south.

Sapporo

Niigata

Hiroshima
Kitakyushu
Fukuoka

Kyoto

Tokyo
Kawasaki
Yokohama

Nagoya
Osaka
Kobe

Kagoshima

▲ Shinkansen locomotives are powered by electricity via overhead cables and connectors. (A shinkansen train appears in the photograph on the book cover.)

People on the move

In the big cities, trains rather than buses are the main means of public transport. Taxis are useful in an emergency, but are expensive. The biggest cities, such as Tokyo, Osaka, Nagoya, Sapporo and Kyoto, have underground railways. Well over 7 million people use the Tokyo underground every day. Bicycles and motorcycles are popular in cities, as well as in the country.

By sea and air

Regular ferry services operating between the islands take in the more remote locations, such as Okinawa. Domestic airlines also provide flights to outlying regions as well as to towns on Honshu and the bigger islands. Japan's seven international airports include Kansai, which was built on reclaimed land in Osaka Bay. Some 8,000 vessels, among them passenger ships, ocean-going cargo ships and oil tankers, make up Japan's merchant fleet.

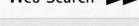

Web Search ▶▶

▶ http://www.japanrail.com/
Japan Railways Group website. Details of rail services and routes.

▶ http://www.jal.co.jp/en/
Website of Japan Airlines, the national carrier.

▶ http://www.stat.go.jp/english/data/nenkan/1431–10.htm
Japanese government site giving statistical tables on different forms of transport.

▶ http://www.mlit.go.jp/english/index.html
Home page of Japan's Ministry of Land, Infrastructure and Transport.

Education

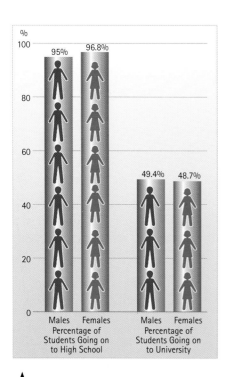

More than 95 per cent of all students progress to high school – though slightly fewer males than females. Just under half of all high-school graduates continue with their education. Male students who begin four-year university courses slightly outnumber females, but many more women than men enrol for two-year courses at junior colleges.

Students in a language class. They are wearing headphones to listen to foreign-language tapes and to communicate with the teacher. ►►

Children must go to school from the ages of 6 to 15. Nearly all of them attend state schools, which are free of charge. Most students then continue their studies for another three years at high school. About half of all those graduating from high school enrol at a university, but many more go on to junior college.

The school year begins in April and is divided into three, or sometimes two, terms. Boys and girls aged 6 to 12 attend elementary school together. They are taught arithmetic, science, social studies, music and physical education. They also study the Japanese language and learn calligraphy – the art of writing Japanese characters. They learn how to cook and to sew. Normally, each class has between 30 and 40 students.

The school day

School usually starts at about 8.30 in the morning and finishes at 3.00 or 3.30 in the afternoon. There are short breaks between lessons and a longer break of about an hour at lunchtime. At the end of every day groups of students clean their classrooms, the hallways, the playground and the toilets. Classes run from Monday to Friday and on some Saturday mornings.

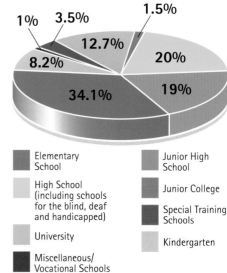

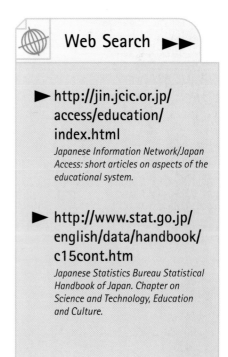

From kindergarten to university – pie chart showing percentages of students of all ages at all types of educational establishments in Japan.

Pie chart legend:
- Elementary School
- Junior High School
- High School (including schools for the blind, deaf and handicapped)
- Junior College
- University
- Special Training Schools
- Miscellaneous/Vocational Schools
- Kindergarten

Pie chart percentages: 1%, 3.5%, 1.5%, 12.7%, 20%, 8.2%, 19%, 34.1%

Teacher and pupils in an elementary school class. Teaching is formal, with all pupils sitting at desks, and boys and girls in the same class.

High school and university

To progress from elementary school to middle, or junior high, school, students must know how to read and write about 1,000 *kanji* – the Chinese characters used in Japanese. At junior high school, they begin to study English and learn to play a traditional Japanese musical instrument. Students are expected to dress smartly and many schools require them to wear uniforms.

To gain a place at high school, after junior high, students must pass an entrance examination. So, too, must high-school graduates wishing to go on to university. Competition for places at the best high schools and universities is fierce and the examinations are hard. Many students sit their entrance examinations more than once before they pass.

Web Search ▶▶

▶ http://jin.jcic.or.jp/access/education/index.html
Japanese Information Network/Japan Access: short articles on aspects of the educational system.

▶ http://www.stat.go.jp/english/data/handbook/c15cont.htm
Japanese Statistics Bureau Statistical Handbook of Japan. Chapter on Science and Technology, Education and Culture.

Sport and Leisure

Baseball and football are popular in Japan alongside traditional sports such as sumo wrestling and judo.

Many Japanese are sports fans or enjoy taking part in sports themselves. Team games, including basketball and volleyball, are played by many people all over the country. Individual sports and leisure activities, such as swimming, golf, skiing and fishing, are also very popular.

Sumo wrestling is more than 2,000 years old. From the age of 15, the wrestlers, who are all male, follow a special diet and training routine to put on weight. Some weigh as much as 200 kilograms. The contests are fought on a straw mat known as a ring. At the start of the bout, the two contestants, wearing a loincloth with a thick belt, throw salt into the ring. This ritual comes from the Shinto religion and symbolizes purification. To win the bout, a contestant must force his opponent out of the ring or make him fall down.

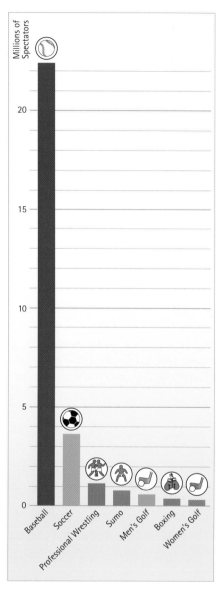

Numbers of spectators at events each year in Japan, by sport.

◄◄ A baseball game between schools in Kyoto.

21

Martial arts and football

Whereas sumo wrestling is largely a spectator sport, other sports based on Japanese traditional martial arts are practised more widely. Judo, karate and kendo (pole fighting in armour), for example, are very popular not only in Japan but in many other countries, too.

Japan has a professional football league and many fine stadiums. In 2002, Japan co-hosted the World Cup competition with its neighbour South Korea. The final was played at the biggest football ground in Japan, Yokohama's International Stadium, which can hold 70,564 spectators. The stadium has a giant display screen measuring 19 metres across. Another huge stadium, the Sapporo Dome on Hokkaido, can quickly change its surface to convert from a football pitch to a baseball pitch.

Baseball has an even bigger following than football, and is widely played in schools. It was introduced by the Americans when they occupied Japan in 1945, at the end of World War II. Golf is the biggest sport in terms of the number of players, of whom there are some 14 million.

▲ Sumo wrestling opening ceremony at the Kokugikan sumo hall in Tokyo. The contestants parade around the competition ring.

Web Search ►►

► www.jinjapan.org/today/ society/society4.html
Japan Information Network article on sports and leisure.

► www.jinjapan.org/ kidsweb/japan/e.html
Kidsweb Japan information on sports.

► www.sg.emb-japan.go.jp/ JapanAccess/sports.htm
Japan Access page on sports.

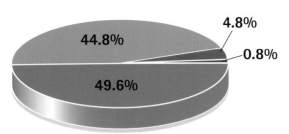

4.8%

44.8%

0.8%

49.6%

■ Shinto ■ Buddhism

■ Others ■ Christianity

◄◄ The relative strength of the different religions in Japan, shown as a percentage of population.

Armed Forces

After World War II (1939–45), Japan vowed not to make war on other countries. Today, Japan's armed forces are known as the Self-Defence Forces. In a country of 127 million people, only some 235,000 are in the military. The biggest force is the army, which has about 150,000 soldiers.

▶▶ Ornate float at the Gion festival in Kyoto. Portable Shinto shrines are paraded through the streets.

Most towns have open-air markets, where local farmers bring their produce and people buy meat, fruit and vegetables. ▼

Daily Life and Religion

Japan is a prosperous country where most people enjoy a good standard of living. Health services are excellent. Life expectancy is the highest in the world. Many people lead modern lifestyles but follow traditional religions.

The brightly lit city centres, where many people work, are full of tall modern buildings housing company offices, expensive apartments and fashionable shops. Cars, buses, taxis and motorcycles fill the streets.

Businesses normally open on weekdays from 9.00 in the morning till 5.00 in the evening. Many offices stay open much later and some shops also open on Saturdays. But the Japanese work fewer hours a week, on average, than the British, the Americans or some Europeans.

Clothing

Most Japanese people wear western-style clothing – whether business suits in the office or jeans and trainers outside business hours. However, at festival times, such as New Year, or at weddings, men and women often dress up in the traditional kimono. This is a beautiful brightly coloured embroidered silk robe that wraps around the body and is tied with a sash.

Weddings and funerals

Couples getting married usually like to have a Shinto wedding ceremony. Shinto is an ancient religion found only in Japan. It is based on the worship of ancestors and nature. Shinto shrines are to be found in homes and all over Japan, even on top of Mount Fuji.

For funerals, it is traditional to have a Buddhist ceremony. Buddhism is a religion that reached Japan some 1,500 years ago from India.

Arts and Media

I n Japan today traditional performing arts flourish alongside modern, award-winning Japanese cinema. Japanese folk music festivals draw large crowds, as do rock concerts and western classical music. Japan's newspapers have the highest readership in the world.

Bunraku puppet theatre is more than 400 years old. The puppets are large and lifelike, and each one is worked by a team of three puppeteers. A narrator recounts the plot, to the accompaniment of music played on a *shamisen*, a traditional kind of banjo.

Like bunraku, *kabuki* theatre began centuries ago and is still popular today. The performers are traditionally men, who, with painted faces and wearing colourful costumes, act out the dramas in a specially exaggerated style.

Newspapers

The Japanese buy some 70 million newspapers every day, and some 750 million books and 3,500 million magazines in a year. The *Yomiuri Shimbun* is the world's best-selling newspaper, selling nearly 15 million copies daily.

Television is much preferred to radio. Japanese people watch about three and half hours a day, on average, but listen to only about 40 minutes of radio. NHK, the Japanese Broadcasting Corporation, is publicly funded.

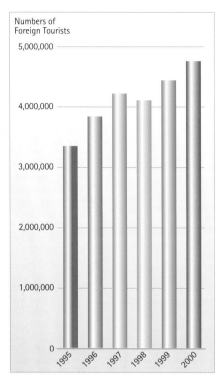

▲ Numbers of foreign tourists visiting Japan, where tourism is a big industry.

◄◄ Japanese children playing video games. Japanese companies such as Nintendo and Sony are leaders in this market.

Japanese cinema

Japanese cinema has become famous through directors such as the late Akira Kurosawa and, more recently, Shohei Imamura and Takeshi Tikano. Since the 1950s Japanese films have won awards at Cannes, Venice and other international film festivals. In Japan, animated cartoon films are popular. Often these are based on cartoons found in manga – comic books that are widely read by Japanese adults and children alike.

A street video screen. Japan is a world-leader in audio-visual technology. ▶▶

Most Japanese radio and television broadcasting stations are paid for through advertising. The number of subscribers to cable TV has nearly trebled to 21.5 million in 10 years. ▼

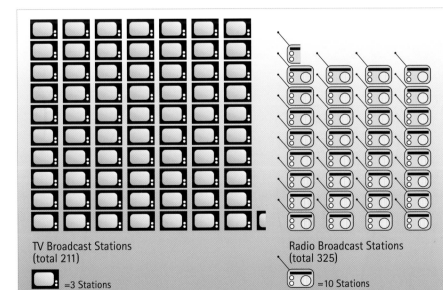

TV Broadcast Stations
(total 211)

▭ =3 Stations

Radio Broadcast Stations
(total 325)

▭ =10 Stations

Web Search ▶▶

▶ http://www.broadcast-live.com/japan.html
Listen to live radio broadcasts from Japan.

▶ http://www.kyoto-su.ac.jp/information/famous/
Kyoto Sangyo University site about famous people in Japan.

▶ http://jin.jcic.or.jp/arts.html
Japanese Information Network (JIN) with links to articles and data on the arts, performing arts, music and film.

Government

Japan has an emperor, but his presence is symbolic and he has no real power. The people are governed by the Diet, or parliament, which is also the country's law-making body.

A written constitution, drawn up in 1947, guarantees the Japanese people freedom of speech, freedom of the press and freedom of religious practice.

The Diet consists of the House of Representatives (*Shugiin*) and the House of Councillors (*Sangiin*). The Shugiin is the more powerful of the two, and its members can overturn decisions made in the Sangiin. Elections to the Shugiin are held every four years. Anyone aged 20 or over may vote and at 25 may stand for election.

Prefectures

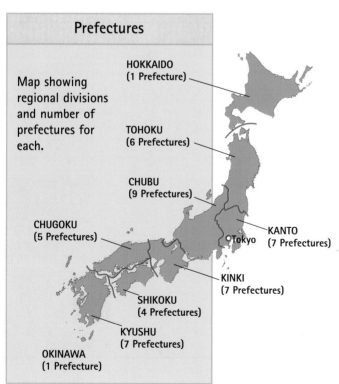

Map showing regional divisions and number of prefectures for each.

HOKKAIDO
(1 Prefecture)

TOHOKU
(6 Prefectures)

CHUBU
(9 Prefectures)

CHUGOKU
(5 Prefectures)

KANTO
(7 Prefectures)

Tokyo

KINKI
(7 Prefectures)

SHIKOKU
(4 Prefectures)

KYUSHU
(7 Prefectures)

OKINAWA
(1 Prefecture)

The Diet building in Tokyo. ▶▶

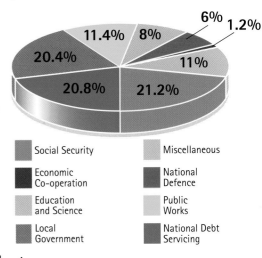

6% 1.2%
11.4% 8%
20.4%
11%
20.8% 21.2%

Social Security | Miscellaneous
Economic Co-operation | National Defence
Education and Science | Public Works
Local Government | National Debt Servicing

Allocation of government spending.

Electoral regions and districts

Three hundred of the Shugiin's 480 members are elected to represent each of 300 electoral districts. The remaining 180 seats are allocated to the different political parties, after elections across the country's 11 electoral regions. In each region, the party gaining the most votes gets the highest number of seats, the party coming second the next highest, and so on. This is known as proportional representation.

The Diet in session.

The prime minister and Cabinet

The Sangiin has 242 members of whom 94 are elected by proportional representation, and 148 as representatives of Japan's 47 prefectures (see map). Elections for half the seats are held every 3 years and members serve for 6 years.

The leader of the party that wins most seats in the Shugiin usually becomes the prime minister. The prime minister then appoints the members of his Cabinet, with the consent of the Diet. The Cabinet puts into effect all the policies agreed by the Diet, for example on public spending, taxation, law and order and foreign affairs.

Web Search ▶▶

▶ http://www.stat.go.jp/ english/data/nenkan/ 1431-18.htm
Japanese government site giving statistical tables on spending on health and welfare.

▶ http://www.stat.go.jp/ english/data/nenkan/ 1431-22.htm
Japanese government site giving statistics on government and elections.

▶ http://www.polisci.com/ almanac/nations/nation/ JA.htm
Political Reference Almanac's data and other information on Japanese government and politics.

▶ http://jin.jcic.or.jp/ business.html
Japanese Information Network (JIN) with links to articles and data on taxation and government spending.

Chronology of Historical Events: 660 BCE to CE 1951

660 BCE
Jimmu Tenno becomes first emperor

CE 1192–9
Rule of Minamoto-no-Yoritomo, the country's first shogun (military dictator)

1639
Under shogun Tokugawa Ieyasu, Japan shuts off from the West for 200 years

1853
US Navy Commodore Matthew Perry sails into Tokyo Bay to break Japan's isolation from western countries

1858
Japan signs trade treaties signed with USA, UK, France and others

1867–8
Defeat of the last shogun and restoration of imperial rule under Emperor Meiji

1890
Setting up of the first Diet

1904–5
Victory over Russia in Russo-Japanese War establishes Japan as the strongest military power in Asia

1931
Japan occupies Manchuria in China and in 1937 starts war with China

1941
Japan enters World War II on the side of Germany, after bombing US Navy base at Pearl Harbor, Hawaii

1945
US aircraft drop atomic bombs on Hiroshima and Nagasaki, destroying the cities and forcing Japan's surrender. US troops occupy Japan

1947
Japan adopts new constitution and renounces war

1951
Peace Treaty signed with USA and 47 other countries

Place in the World

In the past 60 years Japan has emerged from the devastation of war and foreign occupation to take its place as one of the strongest economies and leading trading nations in Asia and the world.

In 1945, when Japan surrendered at the end of World War II, much of the country lay in ruins. Two cities in particular, Hiroshima and Nagasaki, were completely destroyed, after US warplanes dropped atomic bombs on them. Some 340,000 people were killed outright in the attacks or died within days from radiation burns caused by the explosions.

Occupation

For the next six years, Japan was occupied by US troops and underwent major reforms. The emperor, who had once been considered divine, was stripped of his powers and given purely ceremonial duties. The Diet alone became responsible for governing the country.

The original castle at Nagoya was built by the shogun Tokugawa Ieyasu in 1612. A concrete replica now stands in its place. ▼

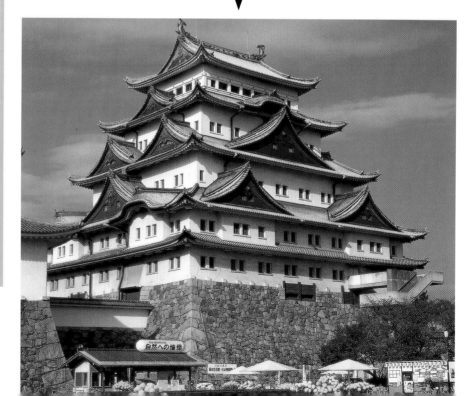

Reconstruction

In the following years, Japan rebuilt its industries to concentrate much of its effort on producing and selling high-technology goods. Since 1983, Japan has had the highest balance of trade surplus in the world. Japan's principal trading partner is the USA.

In the late 1990s, the Japanese economy suffered as a result of an economic downturn in Asian countries where Japanese banks and financial companies had made heavy investments. However, today Japan still has the third-largest economy in the world, after the USA and China.

▲ The ruined dome at the centre of the atom-bomb explosion in Hiroshima.

Imports and exports of major products for the year 2000. When the value of exports is higher than the value of imports, this is called a balance of trade surplus. ▼

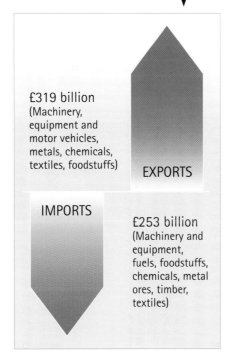

£319 billion (Machinery, equipment and motor vehicles, metals, chemicals, textiles, foodstuffs)

EXPORTS

IMPORTS

£253 billion (Machinery and equipment, fuels, foodstuffs, chemicals, metal ores, timber, textiles)

DATABASE

Chronology of Historical Events: 1952 to present-day

1952
Japan regains full independence, after withdrawal of US troops

1956
Japan becomes a member of the United Nations

1960s
Thanks to rapid industrial growth, Japan records the world's third-highest gross national product figures

1973
Japanese industry hit by soaring oil prices due to Middle East war

1983
Japan for the first time has the largest trade surplus in the world

2000
Financial crisis affects major banks, insurance companies and others

2002
Japan, along with South Korea, holds the World Cup football competition

Web Search ►►

► http://www.meti.go.jp/ english/policy/index_ tradeinformation.html
Website of Japan's Ministry of Economy, Trade and Industry.

► http://jin.jcic.or.jp/ history.html
Japanese Information Network (JIN) with links to articles on all periods of Japan's history.

Area:
377,719 sq km

Population:
126.8 million

Capital city:
Tokyo (population of central 23 wards: 8.1 million)

Other major cities:
Yokohama (3.4 million), Osaka (2.6 million), Nagoya (2.1 million), Sapporo (1.8 million)

Longest river:
Shinano (367km)

Highest mountain:
Fuji (3,776m)

Currency:
Yen

Flag:
The red circle represents the sun. The Japanese call their flag Hinomanu, which means 'sun disc'. They call their country Nippon, which roughly translates as 'Land of the Rising Sun'. A flag design with the sun has been used as Japan's national symbol for at least four centuries.

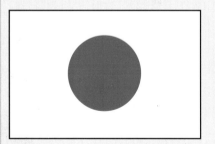

Languages:
Official language: Japanese

Natural resources:
Very small amounts of oil, natural gas, coal, iron, zinc, copper, lead, tungsten, silver, gold

Major exports:
Electrical and other machinery, consumer electronics, precision instruments, motor vehicles, ships and transport equipment, chemicals, iron and steel, metal goods, textiles, foodstuffs

Some national holidays and festivals:
Oshogatsu (New Year)
(End December to 3 January) A time for family reunions. People decorate their houses with pine sprigs and bamboo, eat symbolic food, such as toshi-koshi noodles for a long life, and visit temples and shrines.
Kodomo-no-hi (Children's Day)
(5 May). Families and children fly carp-shaped banners or plastic fish, representing strength, in their gardens.
Tanabata (Star Festival)
(7 July) The one day in the year when two lovers that are stars in the sky are said to meet. People hang out bamboo poles with poems and wishes written on strips of paper.
Obon (13–15 August)
Celebration of the temporary return (for three days) of the spirits of the ancestors. People leave food out for them and clean their gravestones. There

are also firework displays and dancing.
Sports Day (Second Monday in October) A national holiday to celebrate the anniversary of the opening of the Olympic Games held in Tokyo in 1964.
Schichi-go-san ('seven-five-three') (15 November) Girls aged 3 and 7 and boys aged 5, dressed up in kimonos, are taken to their local shrine to pray for good health.

Official religion:
None

Other religions:
Shinto 49.6%, Buddhist 44.8%, Christian 0.8%, others 4.8%

Glossary

BALANCE OF TRADE
The difference in value between goods sold abroad (exports) and goods purchased from abroad (imports).

BONSAI
A method of cultivating trees or shrubs by confining the roots, so that the plants remain very small even when fully grown.

CALLIGRAPHY
The art of using brush strokes to write Chinese or Japanese characters.

CONSTITUTION
A list of principles, drawn up by a state, that sets out the powers and duties of the government and the rights and freedoms of the people.

DIET
The Japanese parliament, consisting of two Houses, an upper and a lower. *See* Sangiin and Shugiin.

ECONOMY
The basis on which a country's wealth is organized.

GROSS NATIONAL PRODUCT (GNP)
The value of goods and services that the people of a country produce over a period.

KANJI
The Chinese characters that are part of the written Japanese language. Unlike letters of the alphabet, they do not represent sounds, but words and ideas.

KENDO
A sport in which opponents wearing protective clothing and masks attempt to strike each with a bamboo pole. The poles represent swords. *See* martial arts.

KIMONO
The traditional Japanese robe, which is worn by both men and women, but nowadays mostly on special occasions.

MARTIAL ARTS
Sports based on traditional fighting techniques. Karate and judo were both developed from forms of unarmed combat. Kendo derives from the sword fighting methods of Japanese warriors called *samurai*.

NIPPON
Japanese for 'Japan'– what Japanese people call their own country.

ORIGAMI
Making models by folding paper. Even complicated shapes, such as animals or birds, can be made using a single square of paper.

PREFECTURE
A political division of Japan. The country is divided into 47 prefectures, each of which has its own local government.

SANGIIN
The House of Councillors, or upper house, of the Japanese parliament. *See* Diet.

SHINKANSEN
Japan's 'bullet train' – an express railway service that covers much of the country.

SHINTO
Japan's traditional religion, based on ancestor worship and belief in the existence of spirits in nature.

SHOGUN
Japanese warlord. Shoguns ruled Japan from the late-13th to late-19th centuries.

SHUGIIN
The House of Representatives, or lower house, of the Japanese parliament. *See* Diet.

SUMO
A traditional sport in which two very large contestants try to push each other out of a ring or throw each other onto the mat.

TSUNAMI
A gigantic wave, usually caused by an earthquake, that washes onto the shore with tremendous force.

TYPHOON
A violent, spiralling wind that can do great damage when it hits land. It is also called a hurricane.

Index